# AN INSIDER'S BOOK

## OR

## How to Read Poetry in one "Easy" lesson.

## by

## Arthur Rider

# Introduction

What is a poem? A poet once said that a poem is a window into the soul. I have found that profound statement to be true for many reasons.

A songwriter may write lyrics for money. But reading the words can tell what the person is like. The Bible says "As a man thinketh in his heart, so is he."-Proverbs 23:7 Poetry then is what is written from the heart. It doesn't matter how well it is covered up with words that rhyme, the poet's mind is exposed. In fact, Life itself can be a poem.

In that thought, this book is divided into several sections. But a poem doesn't have to rhyme to have meaning. Some other famous poets write their poetry in such a way it can almost be called prose. Despite what the critics say, all that a poem has to do is to connect words together to have meaning. That, to me, is a Poem!

About the Author:
The author of this work has written material for various newspapers and magazines, published some poetry, as well as a biblical treatise. He has written over one thousand poems, some of which were compiled into his first poetry book, and given away as a gift for various functions. In addition, he has composed and arranged over one hundred pieces of music, all donated to various schools and charitable organizations. He is currently living in Texas, and is working on a Master's Degree in Education, while working on other books. Otherwise, he works for a living.

Legal Mumbo Jumbo:
At no time should there be an attempt to find profound words of wisdom in this book, nor should there be an attempt to copy without permission. Shame on you for even thinking of doing so.

ISBN:
978-1-4303-0229-2

# Table of Contents

# Section A

# <u>About Poetry</u>

# Poetry For Beginners

So you want to be a poet?
But you don't know how to do it?

It's really easy too,
Now here is what you do:

You just pick a simple theme
Then add a simple rhyme scheme.

But if you don't have the time
You don't really have to rhyme.

Find words that you can depend
And first put them at the end.

You find a phrase that will fit
And so voila! That is it!

And before you know it
You are now a poet!

# What Is A Poem?

What is a poem?
Someone might ask.
This poem is my answer,
And also my task.

A poem can be short.
A poem can also be very, very long.
Does it have to rhyme?
No, not all the time.

A poem can be formal.
It can have structure.
It can also be abnormal,
And be free.

A poem can be an epic
Or a simple limerick.

An Ode, a Ballad, Sonnet, Haiku, or a lyric.
Each of these is a poem.
Classic words flow unbidden
With emotions unfettered
And thoughts unfurled.

What is a poem?
Make it up as you go along,
You can't make a poem wrong.

# What Can A Poem Be Like?

What can a poem be like?
It can be sad.
It can be mad.
It can be glad.
It can be rad.

It can go dark,
going to the park,
or having a lark
as it makes its' mark.

The words twist and turn.
It hurts like a burn.
It can make you spurn,
as you hope to learn.

A poem may rhyme.
But not all the time.
It doesn't cost a dime,
For a lemon or a lime.

It can be very short and sweet,
or a long ode's your treat
As you wait around to meet
Singing a song with a beat.

What can a poem be like?
That's what a poem is like.

# Who Can Be A Poet?

Can a poet be normal
To write things so formal?
Can it be that one has to be
Slightly off, just watch and see.

Who else talks to oneself in rhyme?
And surrounds paper with words all the time?
A poet is two people without a doubt
A private and public persona fighting it out.

It doesn't matter what you write
Iambic pentameter, or an ode form so tight
That words are hard, flipped like a card
Or oozed out of a brain full of lard.

How do I know this to be true?
Did you notice a poet is talking to you?
Did you notice the poetic style
That sticks out like a mile?

So if you don't mind being whacked
Or just a little bit cracked
Then poetry writing will be the thing
To provide therapy to the craziness you bring.

You don't have to be crazy to write
But it helps when you're in the fight
To put words down, with a smile or frown
With verb form, an adjective or a noun
To end up a poet with renown.

So what makes a person a poet?
If you can write it, then you know it!

# A Poem

It's there,
I know it is.
Somewhere deep,
Deep inside, in the midst
Of all other emotions
Thriving on them.
I know it's there
Devouring all the pain
Absorbing all the happiness.
Waiting to breathe,
Yearning to live.
It's there.
I know it is.

# Writer's Block

I sit here staring at a blank sheet
I think and think but I've got a block.
Stress is increasing my heartbeat
And my brain feels dead as a rock.

I want to do something great
Or at least somewhat swell,
But I feel that it's too late
My creativity has hit a dry well.

I then realize my trouble
The curse that writers fear.
Thoughts now burst like a bubble
And my mind slips out of gear.

What is it that puts us into a spin,
watching time creep by on the clock?
I realize that I can now begin
I just had that old writer's block.

"Hey now!" I start to think
"Why not write about my brain lock,
And not just make a stink
Worrying about that silly writer's block?"

But then as I start to write
I begin again to feel a stall.
My writer's block starts to fight
Hitting my bloodied face into the wall.

It then threw me to the ground
This was getting rough!
After it gave me such a pound
I knew I'd had enough!

As I sat there bruised and stunned
I wondered what I should do.

I realized that I was outgunned,
I knew when I was through.

As I cleaned up from the mess
I decided it's not worth it.
This is something I confess
That I just want to forget it.

So if you're thinking what to write
And you feel you're sinking into rock,
It's pointless to start a fight
With that old meanie, Writer's Block.

So if you ever have writer's block
Here's some advice for you.
Take a break, get off the clock
Or it'll beat you, too.

So give the block its' due
Just hang in there and grin,
And when it's through with you
You can write again.

# How To Rhyme

I can teach you how to rhyme.
You just need to fill in the blank.
It just takes a little T _ _ E (hint: a clock tells it!)
and you can put it in the B _ _ K!(hint: put money in it.)

As you work to make your plan,
For the day or for the night,
In hopes of gaining a F _ N(hint: keeps you cool.)
Prepare to start the F _ _ _ _ T!(hint: a brawl.)

You just make a running start,
And see what you can do.
Just work out each single P _ _ T(hint: a piece of something.)
To work a rhyme or T _ O.(hint: more than one.)

Now you go ahead and try it yourself,
Go ahead and make another rhyme.
Don't place your skill upon a S _ _ _ F(hint: a cabinet spot to put things.)
Use your talent all the T _ _ E!(hint: a clock tells it!)

# My Sonnet On A Sonnet

What is a Sonnet?
A Poem that the English write,
Classical as a bonnet,
And always strict and also right.

Three Quatrains start the mark.
A couplet then comes not to diminish
A genteel walk in the park
To make the rhyme scheme then finish.

While Italians write this too
Shakespeare does this writing better
The writing style stays true
And sounds swell despite rhyme's fetter

So now you can therefore see
This is a sonnet to me.

# Ode To My Memory

I write this to you, my fading friend.
I wander the streets, I go end to end,
I stretch up to the ceiling, and to the couch lowly bend.
I search for you, and there's not a penny I wouldn't spend.

I once thought that I would never forget what life brings
But as I got older, I started to forget so many things.
Where once life brought so much joy that my memory sings
There is now only the absence, which so painfully stings.

My memory once brought back so much joy
I felt like I was playing with a favorite toy.
But now my memory plays so very coy
And I forget what it was like to be a boy.

What I once could hear and see
I forgot what it was to be.
What was it like climbing a tree?
Will you remember to come back to me?

I once went out so very bold
But now everything is on hold.
I wanted so much to break out of the mold
But now I can't remember what I had be told.

I so wanted to be friends with you
But memory, you haven't been true.
What fine places have you been to,
Without you I wouldn't know what to do.

I would write you a nice song
Would it be so wrong?
It might not take very long
After all, we both belong.

My memory, you are very dear
Please don't make me feel drear
Or even have to shed a single tear.
Stay with me, please stay near.

I would remind you of all the fun
Of all the things that we have done.
I remember the time we had to run.

Someone was looking for us with a gun.

I want to keep you with me
I do want to always see.
If you could stay and always be
I won't tie you down, you will be free.

This Ode is o'er
I won't be a bore
While you may choose the door
You'll still be my core.

# Haiku

Poetic Order
Now put into great feeling
Sense with emotion

# Haikulikeahoo

Poetry
Some words
They may rhyme
Not all the time
This is my Haiku Poem.
A different type of poetic form.
Just count the words now.
They tell you how
A simple form.
Try it.
Poetry.

# Section B

# Friendship And Love

# A Friend

What is so precious
and is so sweet,
that makes one feel
without one incomplete?

The answer of course,
is a friend.

A friend is that One,
that Pearl of great price.
That friend is the One,
to you is very nice.

A friend is rare
in a world of people,
acquaintances don't stand out
like a friend as a steeple.

How lucky a person is
when one can count a friend
through all the storms of life,
depend on to the end.

What can I say
so your ear can bend,
and see that golden smile?
I love you, Friend.

# What Is Friendship?

What is friendship?
Is it a smile to fill in the hours,
or hugs to override the powers?
Is it a nameless feeling that comes and goes,
or a sense of duty fighting common foes?
Is it a sense of humor to laugh and sing,
or comfort to one who suffers death's sting?
Is it looking your friend eye to eye
or at their side when they die?
Is it really anything,
or is it everything?
I will be your friend.
Will you be my friend?

# Thoughts On Friendship

What is Friendship?
Is it a feeling?
Is it a sense of connection
And a sense of revealing?

It is all that.
It is also more.
It is something that touches,
yea the heart at its' very core.

This is my promise.
A friendship that is true.
For all the blessings given me
I will share them all with you.

# Note To A Sick Friend

I just wanted you to know
I'm sorry you're not feeling well
I hope you'll soon feel aglow
And start to feeling swell.

It's just a note to say I missed you,
It's just a little rhyme to say,
I hope you'll be good as new
And may this cheer your day!

No, I'm not a doctor at all,
But laughter is medicine, too.
There's no pharmacist you need to call,
Only smile while reading this through.

My time is gone and done
So I'll just close to say,
May ill times turn to fun
And may you have a great day.

# Looking For My Friends

The world is cold.
Many look to take advantage,
They look for number one.
That is their adage.

But those that I trust,
those are loyal and just.
Those that have stayed in
Through both thick and thin.

They keep their promise to me.
This is what I see,
They will be with me,
until the very end.

They always remember my birthday.
They always know what to say.
For my own good and joy they stay.
Are you looking for my friends, too?

# Friendship

May this poem I write this day
Help in what I need to say,

Please believe what is said is true
I hold my heartfelt friendship close to you.

I pray that as we grow together
That our friendship will last forever.

As the words flow from heart to heart
And we share each of us a part,

We tie ourselves to Christ's word
Living according to what we've heard.

This thought is deeper than it sounds
My care for you knows no bounds.

May the Lord guide us, dear friend
To a beautiful place that has no end.

Though we are different in a way,
We can count on our friendship to stay.

There are so many things that we share
Including God's love which is more than fair,

You taught me to be patient and kind,
These things I will always keep in mind.

Our humor calms the soul like balmy weather
And our trust makes burdens feel like a feather.

May these lines I've said help you to see
How much you will always mean to me.

# Fountain Of Friendship

Come let us drink from the fountain of friendship.
Let us refresh ourselves in it's fine spray.
Let us walk in the lovely garden it waters
and stay there all the day.

Come let us climb the tree of life
and play together in time's sand.
Let us thank our God for friends
who often lend us a hand.

While we live and while we breathe,
Let us never forget to say and do
kind things to our friends
who have been to us so true.

# Thoughts On Loving Someone

Time with her stands still
My voice fails at her sight
I open my faltering self to her.
I tell of my hopes, my dreams, and wishes.
She tells of her aims, her goals, her plans.
I want to know more about her.
A dear Christian sister,
I'd never want to hurt her.

Her soft tresses float gently like leaves in a forest pond in autumn,
I long to touch her soft hair, to know that she is there,
To feel that she really cares.

Her hair is like a summer's field waving in the breeze.
Her eyes are like clear cool pools of water.
Her voice is like the gentle cooing of a dove.
Her smile is like a ray of sunshine.
Her face is like that of an angel.
Her walk floats so that not a blade of grass is injured.

I remember her gentle laugh
A peace that calms my heart's storm
Her singing brings thoughts of an angel in disguise.

These thoughts of love for her,
I would be a friend for her,
I'd give all I had for her,
I'd do anything for her,
I would go anywhere for her.
I wonder if she would let me?

# Thoughts Of Love

As the crickets serenade me, my thoughts are turning to you.
My love's grown strong as an oak but I still don't know what to do.

As the stars guide the sailors on the sea,
I pray they also guide your heart to me.

You are a rose, with thorns, tough and sharp as much.
But your fragile petals beg for a gentler touch.

The light post of life guides me to wonderful springs of joy.
I wish to take you there, when you're happy I'm again a playful
boy.

The boy in the man wishes to not play Red Light, Green Light.
He's tired of it now, not reaching you while having you in sight.

I try to think of other things, but in everything I still see you.
The flowers remind me and places we've been also haunt me too.

Questions race through my mind: What can I do to please you?
Could you love me back? if so, what do you wish me to do?

Before, life had a dull, limited purpose for me, a meandering bug.
But now life is so complete, when you give me a precious hug!

I don't want to hurt you; just to be free to love you is all I ask.
I thought it best for you for me to forget you but I failed in my
task.

Wherever I walk, it seems I can see you by my side.
No matter what I do, no matter how hard I tried.

The monument of my Love still stands, it's too strong, forever I
will love you.
Long ago my dreams found you, led me to you, to a love that's
pure and true.

Loving you is not easy, I work hard for just your smile.
But I've found that life without you is an even tougher trial.

I don't need much from you, and I'd gladly the price would pay.
I just want you to love me; I've loved you every day.

Just tell me those sweet words to my waiting ears.
Tell me we can be together through our remaining years.

If it's possible for you to do this, to really say that it's true,
I'd be happy to do more to please you, and to love only you.

God made the path that brought me to you and you to me.
All I ask is to follow the path to see what is to be.

As I show these thoughts of love that grew,
There's only one thing left to say: I LOVE YOU.

# In Love

The greatest gift from above
Is to be in love.
In the love of a precious heart
To spread joy everywhere
And to glow within when apart.

In the love of God's son
As he shows peace to all,
And pointing out the goal to be won.

The point of being in love,
Is to be in Christ, having been in God,
And from God above.

Though we were not there by sight,
We believe, through his word
And in faith we spread the light.

Never forget, and don't ever fret.
To be in love is the gift from above.

# Section C

# The Seasons

# The Turning Of The Seasons

Seasons come and seasons go.
Time is in a ceaseless flow.

You're born, you celebrate.
You even get a chocolate cake!

The New Year is brought in.
I wonder where it has been?

What are the real reasons
For the turning of the seasons?

Presidents and mothers on days we remember.
The March of Spring and Autumn September.

Valentine's and weddings share the love,
Bright as sunshine and light as a dove.

Four leaf clovers and Easter eggs
Call out to us, yes and begs.

The summer burns us with its' heat.
Ice cream's cool touch can't be beat!

Patriotic tunes stir the souls,
As flags fly high up in their poles.

Children start going to school,
Crowds all dive into the pool.

Halloween masks and pumpkin faces.
The end is near for time now races.

Giving thanks to Christmas gifts,
Finding hope to mend the rifts.

We finally now come to the Year's end,
The turn of the seasons can now begin.

# A Friend For The Holidays

What can a friend do for a friend?
What can a friend give and send?

The most I can for my friend give
Is simply for me to live
And to be a friend.

What can a friend say and do
To help a friend like you?

I can only be a friend that's true
Otherwise I have no clue
On what to do.

The holidays send both joy and sadness
Sometimes even some madness

But to my dear friend
To eternity's end
I pledge only to your joy!

# Wedding Poem For A Couple

Remember simple times as a child
Happiness was abound
Parents kept you from being wild
And love seemed to be around.

We are God's children you see
For love and happiness can still be
For you two to do God's will
As marriage leads you up God's hill.

Happiness to both is my wish
And while this rhyme is odd
May these rhymes help guide you
In love, trust, obedience also to God.

# Wedding Song

Brother and sister
Husband and wife
Serving God together
Throughout our whole life

And what God in heart
Only in death let us part
On love's journey let's now start
And in heaven sing "How Great Thou Art"

As we become one
We'll walk hands held in hands
Companions, friends, lovers,  family
Throughout time's flowing sands

# A Birthday Greeting To A Female Friend

Time has turned another page.
You've now reached another stage.

This note has been sent,
To celebrate this great event.

And what is this you say
That brings this note your way?

Why, it's your birthday silly girl,
And so why not have a wonderful whirl!

So party hearty, cheer and play,
Go out, have fun, it's your birthday!

And so may this simple note
Try and not to rock the boat.

But only comes to cheer your way
To having  a great and wonderful day!

# A Valentine Gift

As the days go by
My mind begins to fly
As it turns to remember the past.

My heart can see
That this day can be
One to make something special last.

This day is Valentine's
And there are many signs
To make this day such a blast!

I do hope that this day
Will be the best way
To show what such love is so vast.

This poem is short.
It is just the sort
To send this message very fast.

To you is this note
And that's all she wrote
So here's hoping you're not aghast.

 That what is in my heart
 Let it never depart,
 I just wish you'll be my Valentine!

# Summer

As the time flies
My heart sighs
To the beat of wings
All the while it sings
Of Summer!

The peace that comes
Past the beating drums
Telling spring classes,
All of the masses
"It's Summer!"

The breeze goes by
Past the sun up high,
Calling to my heart
Telling it to start
The summer.

Take heart my friend
Of this note I'll send
Telling the spring good-bye
And to the summer "Hi!"
Let's all thank this guy,
Summer!

# Sweetest Day

Happy Sweetest Day
To the sweetest friend I know.
A person with a sweet attitude,
An attitude that you like to show.

Have a happy, special day
It's a calendar date you see,
But I don't need a calendar
To see that you look sweet to me.

How did Sweetest Day happen?
Who chose October Twenty?
Does it really matter?
Just enjoying it is plenty.

So have a terrific Sweetest Day,
And enjoy the whole weekend too.
From a friend who cares a lot
And wishes the best for you.

# Season's Greetings Poem

May the holiday break
With all its' give and take
Find a fine way to make
Its' cheerful way to you.

What is a holiday
Without finding a way
To so cheerfully say
"Have a happy Ho Ho Ho!"

May the holiday season
Cause one to have a reason,
Even with all the teasin'
Its' cheerful way to you.

No stress, no rush
Now calm, now hush.
Ok, now I'll gush!
Happy Holidays to you!

# Section D

# Faith

# Faith

Faith is more than a word.
Faith is more than a feeling.
Faith is more than blind.
Faith is more than seeing.

"What is Faith?" Someone might ask.
What can be done to answer,
Or what can be shown to another
This is now my task.

Does faith require anything from me?
Are there facts to support it to be?
I have no answers of my own
To the Word of God's wisdom, this I will see.

The Book that tells me about faith,
Says that evidence begins the task.
But facts and figures are not alone.
A decision is required, a question is asked.

The Lord goes about "the work of faith"
His Word tells us this is true.
To believe is not alone, it takes faith
To obey and to love, we are to do.

Faith is the foundation, a solid rock.
Without it we will tumble.
The storms of life and stony paths,
Without faith we will stumble.

I hope this message of what is faith
Will help to clear the air.
Faith is more than a word.
It is a life that we are to share.

# Words Of Encouragement

What these words have to say
may it enrich the heart.
This prayer if saying may
help you to never part
from the one and the only.

May I offer part of the sword
and words of encouragement.
May you always stay with the Lord
with heart, soul and knees bent
and with fellowship never be bored.

Words are only words
that attempt this brother's love
to point beyond the flying birds
toward the Father above.

# Oh Come Let Us Sing

Oh come let us sing,
and to God our praises bring.
The Lord came to us by birth.
He was born, He lived upon the earth.

And for us a death He chose,
was buried and then arose.
Indicated by the Spirit,
Oh can you now hear it?

He was seen by angels from on high,
prophesying how He was to die.
Preached among nations oh how true,
believed on in the world by so few.

Manifest by flesh the Word does say.
Taken up in glory, He'll return some day.
Let us praises sing to our Lord the King,
Oh come now let us sing!

# How Precious Is The Word Of Life

How precious is the Word of Life to everyone in sin.
It brings to light the Son of God and shows through Him we win.

The Fount of Love is all we need to quench our thirst of life,
If we seek first the Lord our God then peace will end our strife.

The Love of Saints is praised above and blessed is to care.
The Lord has said, "Go preach the Word" and "Blessed is to share."

The sound of praise is great indeed, to sing holds peace inside.
For music is to love the Lord and show we're on His side.

How precious is the fount of life, how precious is the Light!
We sing God's praise and show His love and preach His word and Might!

# While The Day Is Bright

While the day is bright,
Through the shining light,
Let us do what's right,
With all of our might.

God's promise, don't you see
Is everything that's to be.
He does this for you and me
He works to make us free.

He asks only but one thing,
for us to give Him bring.
Of our worship that we sing
our praises to heaven ring.

He wants for us to love
from here to high above,
Flying to heaven like a dove
He and others we should love.

So let us now to God do
To Him let us be true.
And when life is through
Everything will be made new.

# Life's Gifts

Not worthy of God's Blessings.
Not worthy of God's Love.
Not worthy of God's Power.
Or such gifts from Above.

What is joy without sorrow?
Yesterday without tomorrow?
As time goes by,
We're born, live and die.

What matters in life?
What's a fork without a knife?
A balance is made.
The mountain and the glade.

We are given a choice,
To weep or to rejoice.
I know what I will do.
The choice is up to you.

# The Life That Lingers

The Life that lingers behind the earth
Laughs better, lives longer, and enjoys rebirth.
The Lord shows peace through foggy minds
And love to all people, yes all kinds.

To care for the rich and poor,
The races, colors and the sore.
He cares for woman, child, and man
He truly cares as only He can.

If God can love these souls
Can we but heap coals,
On our enemy by loving all we can,
And show Our Lord the race that we ran.

# As I Lie Here Alone

As I lie here alone
My thoughts and feelings surround me.

I wonder about life and love
My pain and fears surround me.

I run from the thoughts that plague my very soul
I turn to solace from those that I have gone to before
I meditate upon the words that have given me comfort in the past,
And when I think that I have conquered my enemy at last,
My doubts and concerns surround me.

For a brief time I take courage from those whom I care
My friends and family surround me.

When I am with others, I draw on their strength
My shyness fades and I gain courage to go out
I work and walk amid the light of day
And gain strength from the Lord as I pray,
But then my memories and phobias surround me.

Each day comes to confront my own mortality
My life and health surround me.

I want to tell someone that I care for of my love
But the pain of past loss besets me.
I don't want to be alone in this life
But the fears of past hurts return.
When my courage grows weak, my friends help me seek
The peace and joy that surrounds me.

But when I am sick in my bed
The sadness and grief surround me.

Too many things I don't understand
But from what I've learned, I'll trust in the hand

That guides me from the very living Word of God.
I'm told that when I'm weak then am I strong
Because I no longer trust in my own self,
But in someone greater than my fears,
Greater than my pain,
Greater than my friends,
Greater than anything the world brings against me.
I finally feel free of the shackles of life
And now I can finally in faith see,
That hope and love surround me.

As I lie here alone
My thoughts and feelings surround me.

# Let Us Work Together As We Walk

Let us work together as we walk,
The Lord will be with us then
Let's also to strangers talk
Of God's grace from sin.

The Lord is with us when
we're working as we walk.
He told us of Himself
Let's also to strangers talk.


As we travel through life's pathway
Telling of God's great story.
Let us work together as we onward go
Walking the pathways to glory.

# Do You Believe?

"Do You Believe?" I was asked this question.
What do I believe? What is my answer?

I was once an unbeliever. I questioned faith through science.
The facts overwhelmed me, and I was forced to decide my fate.

"Do You Believe?" I was faced with this question.
Old logic had failed me, I had to give an answer.

Science and History, no longer a mystery.
They backed up my now budding faith.

"Do You Believe?" I was given this question.
The facts now gave me my answer.

From an agnostic, a skeptic, a doubter
I came to see, yes I believe!

# Section E

# General Poetry

# My Words

My Words are like stones.
They fly with great effort.
They land with harsh tones.

My words are like fish,
that swim in murky waters.
They sometimes become a dish.

My words are spoken,
and are lightly taken
or hatefully broken.

My words are written.
They can be savored,
or bitterly bitten.

My words are here.
Please listen to the laugh,
then listen to the tear.

How will you react to my words?

# My Pet Rock

People may have pets that bark or purr or even chirp.
My pet rock is too polite to even give a burp.

While folks look for lost pets that may wander away
I don't have to wonder, cuz my pet rock will stay.

While much money is spent to care for a dog or a cat,
My pet saves me enough money to buy me a hat.

My pet doesn't leave a mess for me to clean up after.
I watch other owners fuss and I start my laughter.

My pet rock, I know where you are.
You won't run, you won't chase a car.

So you can keep your fancy pet.
I know I have the best one yet!

# My Dog Ate A Tree

One day I came home to see
My dog had eaten a tree.

It was my mom's six foot pine
That my puppy chose to dine.

When a puppy likes to chew
It could be a sock or a shoe.

When a big dog wants to chew
Who then knows what it will do?

My puppy was six months old
And six feet long, truth be told.

We knew something would happen one day
That would force us to give her away.

We never thought we would ever see
that we would come home to see no tree.

I hear that my puppy is now grown
Happy keeping a farmland mown.

You may not believe it is true.
Why would I ever lie to you?

# What's So Funny?

What is it about humor that's so funny,
That makes us laugh, and comics money?
If I had a dollar for each little joke,
That had people laugh, I'd still be broke.

They say children laugh thousands of times.
They laugh at strange words and silly rhymes.
How many adults can make sense of kids?
I can give odds to how many bids.

How can even a fussy grownup bring
Such a funny thought to such a thing?
What grownup today can give a giggle
When hearing even a silly riddle?

Listen, our inner child still calls out
"Please play with me," it wants to shout.
I'd rather have joy than lots of money.
Look in the mirror, now that is funny!

# Concrete And Trees

Concrete and Trees
That's what one sees,
The hard and soft, the tough and tender.
Grey and green, do you know what I mean?
One is heavy, Lifeless, ignoring
The very essence of life.
The other is light. It glows. It grows.
Because of it, reaching for it.
It reaches a living for it.
 It is it's essence, showing the fruits,
Shading the weary, reflecting the beauty.
One is dead, the other alive.
One stops, the other goes.
Are you concrete, broken by time,
Ravaged by the world?
Or are you a tree, standing despite it,
Pointing the way for others?

# Can Peace Reign?

Can peace reign in this world
of strife, pain, and agony?
No, but only heaven, where is hurled
the troubles away to Hades
and the true entrance is built on a foundation,
so powerful, that only his own strength
could ever destroy it.
But where is this place where peace reigns?
Can it be found, can it be bothered?
No, for only the saints can be found there,
where with God the rents of the mansions are free,
but only from money.
For to have such a place, to receive this grace,
one only has to be a lifelong follower
of Christ, who set our example.
You remember when the angels
flew down to announce him.
John, Apostle of love wrote that
there can be no peace without God.
Justice is no justice without mercy.
How can we know to reach peace?
The mind can only read from the
words of the Creator, to know.

# Beauty

I see the horrible confusion,
that makes the losers so mad.
The quest for outward appearance
leaves many hopefuls quite sad.

Some sow their ideas and their thoughts
and hope that someday they may reap.
Some say beauty is in the eye of the beholder,
and some say it is only skin deep.

True beauty is in the heart,
and not in a person's face.
It's not what's in the complexion
or because of a person's race.

I hope one day that mankind will see
that a beautiful person is in sight,
just to look beyond the skin
to the inside, shining bright.

# Photo Album

A snowy day of long ago.

Relatives long gone,

Memories of days gone by.

People and Places

That once you knew,

Are now just pictures

In a photo album.

What happened to him?

Is she still around?

Events of another time

Captured forever

On the page of a photo album

When things were different.

# The Rushing Time

Time speeds by so fast
you wish it could just last.
One moment you're young and bold,
the next, you're turning old.

The years are marked to see
just look at what used to be.
First birth, then youth,
and now you see the truth.

There was Junior and then High School,
all the summers swimming in the pool,
then on to College to prepare
for graduation, and the memories so rare.

But don't forget to look forward
as you look back through the tears,
Remember always the loving Lord
who sees the same no matter the years.

There is still time to share,
and to show others you care.
Just glance at the past, but don't stare
and keep running to the goal, you're almost there!

# Spur Of The Moment

What makes women tick? What spurs them on?
What do they want? Do they want a moment?
What makes them so mysterious?
Do they want some timeless notions?
What am I to think? Do I plan before going forward
or do something by the spur of the moment?
Do I know what is going on?
or am I just going through the motions?
Do I understand? I wander momentarily.
What spurs on the quest for knowledge?
Why do women have so many shoes?
Why do women have so many lotions?
The great mysteries of life. The mysteries of love.
Time flies by in a spur of the moment.
We are born and then we die.
Still, I don't understand women's emotions.
I spur on to momentary glory. Does life have a story?
A spur can hurt, and so does life. As does an occasion of strife.
Forget the moment, give God your devotions.
Understanding will come later.
Still I wonder,
What makes women tick?

# Pack Rat

Why am I a pack rat?
Why do I have this obsession?
Is there something I should say?
Something worth confession?

I want to store everything.
All that I can see,
I want to keep with me.

It doesn't matter what
A paper clip, a letter.
I keep it, I feel better.

I have thousands of boxes
I've forgotten what is there.
Throw it away? I can't bear!

I may discard the junk. "One day!" I say,
"It'll be that way!"

Why am I a pack rat?
I give up.
I think I'll go pack.

# Anonymous

Who is this anonymous fellow?
Does he whisper or does he bellow?

Perhaps he's not a he but a she.
If she's a she, she can't be a he.
To find out if she's a she and not a he
I will have to wait and see what is to be.

Why is anonymous hiding anyway?
Is his or her name too hard to say?

I think this anonymous might be wise.
Too wise. I have to cut him down to size.

I'll search for this secretive anonymous.
Is he hiding behind that African Hippopotamus?
Or perhaps she is even behind that silly giant platypus?
Come on, tell me where you are, Anonymous!

I searched the world for this stranger.
I even called for a Texas Ranger,
But he told me he's only called when in danger,
And not to go looking for this silly stranger.

I decided to give up the look
And just read a nice book.

Yes, it's written by that amazing wit.
Yes, Anonymous, your name does truly fit!

# Goodbye Poem

We hate to see you go.
We sure will miss you so.

We'll sigh and sigh to say goodbye,
We hate to see you go.

We wish you well, you've sure been swell,
We hate to see you go.

You've sure been great to us.
So pardon if we fuss.

Take good care, you are so fair,
We hate to see you go.

Hi-Dee-Ho, We'll miss you so,
We hate to see you go!

Lightning Source UK Ltd.
Milton Keynes UK
26 November 2009

146797UK00001B/78/A

9 781430 302292